Money

Energy

Mastery

More books by Susan Glusica

Courage Under Siege, Adversity to Victory
Courageous Women Publications, 2017

Jumpstart Your _____, *Vol III; 15 Inspiring Entrepreneurs Share Stories and Strategies on How to Jumpstart Many Areas of Your Life, Business, Relationships, and Health*

K. Sawa Marketing International Inc., 2020

"The way Susan writes in this book, Money Energy Mastery, it feels like she's talking directly to me. Her take on how expansive money energy is and how it flows within us is really enlightening. I am thankful to find that enjoying unapologetic prosperity can be this easy."

~ Katrina Sawa, Speaker, Jumpstart Your Biz Coach
Int'l Bestselling Author (11 books)
CEO of JumpstartYourBizNow.com

"Money Energy Mastery is a great and enjoyable read containing wonderful, practical advice about attracting in your prosperity flow. Susan has a firm grasp of what it takes to get money moving in your life. A wonderful coach and mentor, Susan Glusica is someone I can well recommend to direct and encourage you on your journey to money health."

~ Yvonne Oswald PhD, www.globalwelcome.com

"Money mastery isn't rocket science; it's simply understanding your money energy. If you want to learn how to create the prosperity of your wildest dreams read this book to raise your money consciousness and attract limitless abundance."

~ Tasha Chen, cofounder, Science of Getting Rich Academy

"Get your copy of this elegant little tool for enhancing your relationship with money! It's a quick and fascinating read (it took me less than 2 hours...because I like to digest what I read slowly). "Everything is energy..." as Albert Einstein has reminded us. Every thought, every emotion and every activity involves energy. Money is energy. Our relationship with money is about our own energy of thought and emotion. Susan Glusica has brilliantly outlined and explained the nature of our inherent relationship with money, which brings us face to face with our relationship with our most fundamental beliefs and thoughts. When we become more awake and aware about our own worth, so do we become more abundant in ways that match our thoughts and beliefs - which are a choice.

"Susan's brief manifesto for financial growth and abundance deserves a place of distinction on your "must read" list of books to read immediately."

~ Sheila Pearl, MSW, CLC
Relationship & Recalibration Coach
Author of "Ageless & Sexy" series

The 7 Money Realities

Money

Energy

Mastery

Susan Glusica

Elevate Your Financial Frequency

To my soulmate, mirror, and truest supporter of all time, Vanja. Our marriage, this book, and our lives wouldn't be what they are without all your support and willing sacrifice. I owe you BIG! Here's to continuing to live our best lives together, wherever and whenever that may be.

Table of Contents

Renee Gambino

Foreword

This book is your beginning. A new way for you to think and act into wealth. To become free of the paradigms of mediocrity—that too many suffer unnecessarily through for lifetimes and generations—and take your generosity and legacy to its highest potential.

Wealth, of course, comes in many forms. We are always wealthy. The Universe only knows growth and abundance. You and everyone else are prime candidates for an abundance of money, love, health, courage and peace, but be aware, the Law of Polarity is always in play. The Law of Polarity is best defined by Newton's Third Law of Motion—for every action there is an equal and opposite reaction. With that understanding, an abundance of money, love, health, joy and peace proves that an abundance of lack, judgment, sickness, regret and stress MUST exist. One cannot exist without the other. It's a choice based in science. But not rocket science.

We speak in terms of wanting more, more, more; but act by retracting in distrust of our ability to grow our minds and our money. In that order—if you want it to work. Working the thought strategy of growing your money before your mind will simply leave you stuck right where you are. It's all relative. Doesn't matter if you make $20k a year or $2 million. You may have been taught by example something like, "If I had more money I'd be able to do more, worry less, be more freed up. Things would just be so much easier," OR "As soon as this money comes in or that happens, everything will change." We're always sideways when we go there. The result in that thinking is things go up and down, but in the end remain the same. It's a wash, or, incremental growth at best. That doesn't keep you coming back for more! It sets you up for settling on what you really want because it's just not "realistic."

It's not your fault. You learned that money doesn't grow on trees, someone needs it more than you, someone always has less than you, greed grows when bank accounts grow, don't take risks, safe is safer, only buy what you need, money isn't in line with spirit/God/source, if you want more money work harder, having big money goals is pretentious, remember where you came from and money can't buy you love!

These are fascinating words to live by when there are bills to pay, kids to go to college, homes to buy, investments to be made, nest eggs to nurture, charities to be blessed, dreams to fulfill, generosity to be experienced and positive impacts on humanity to be made. No wonder the majority of the world finds money maddening and elusive! But let's face it, results speak for themselves. The people who say those things aren't writing six- and seven-figure checks to help kids with cancer. But they "wish" they could. Or they say they would, if… they had the money.

Most people are not aware of where they actually stand with money. It can feel like you got the wind knocked out of you when you find out how money grows and flows. It goes against your "let's make this harder than it is," that you got brain-bathed in growing up.

What we do with this awareness is up to us. What it takes to distill your old thinking down in order to gain increases that actually make a difference in your life and the ones you love is a simple, proven, purposeful approach that gets you a positive result.

Results are what keep you coming back! They up your motivation game. Results cause your discomfort with change and receiving to lose its decision-making power over you. Results give you stronger beliefs in your abilities and self-worth. Stronger beliefs in your abilities and self-worth give you shots of courage. Shots of courage drives more action taking. We do much better when we step into a new way of approaching bigger and better with grace. You can grace out as fast as you want, but specific steps are key so you don't trip so hard on the way up!

This is where Susan's methods are key to maximizing your Money Reality. Our reality is our own personal interpretation of who we think and feel we are. So... sky's the limit there! Options are endless and choices are plenty. Susan nails this understanding and points you in the right direction. She is an expert guide on the subject of Money Reality.

The work in this book sets you up to never go backwards or spiraling down a rabbit hole of your own thinking and doing. Once you hit your next level, there's no going back. Most wealthy people who "lose it all" come back with a vengeance. Why? Because they already grew themselves through thinking and doing into a result. This allows them to speed through the resistance to receive, because they know what frequency they need to operate in, where they're going and how to get there. Shortest distance between two points.

This book gives you awareness, a methodology to give you the insight it takes to put your mark on where you really stand with money and practical, daily exercises to begin your journey to more money and more life.

Caution! The exercises are uncomplicated. Your distrust in your ability to receive may be triggered, showing up in good ole fashioned judgment. Remember the beliefs you were given about money? I'd like to add, money is hard to come by, you have to know someone, you need to be lucky, you need to already be in the club, you need to look different, sound different and I bet their family has a lot of money. Yup… those are more of the beliefs locked in our sub-conscious data storage that we'd call "trigger trippers" that throw us into "Magnificent money growth isn't meant for me." The cure for judgment is curiosity. So try it on! I bet money looks great on you!

Stepping into your personal Money Realization journey with Susan's 7 Money Realities discovery helps you to compartmentalize, energize and strategize your way to financial freedom. The beauty of what her method brings is practicality wrapped in deep purpose and connection. She lives by the Laws of The Universe while standing firmly, feet planted, on the earth. Susan has little time or affection for the minutia and excuses of why you're so special that the rules of what really works don't apply to you.

This book and the work that Susan does is for those who have a desire for more, a willingness to step into having more money, and a fire in their heart that's just waiting for the fuel it needs to burn hotter. Her relationship and wizardry with energy is powerful and intoxicating. Her knowledge of a balance sheet is key. That is why she is known as the Unrivaled Realizer.

Welcome to your beginning. I wish you much love and intense prosperity on your journey with Susan.

Renee "The Boss" Gambino
ReneeGambino.com

Money

Energy

Mastery

Chapter One

How I Discovered The 7 Money Realities™

I've always been a fairly spiritual person. Raised by a Lutheran mother and a lapsed Roman Catholic father, my two sisters and I attended Lutheran Sunday School as kids. I remember, however, that as soon as I took Communion, my mother stopped taking us. This is when I had my first crisis of identity. Mother made it clear we "should" go to church, but now it was to be our choice. For her part, Mom had a personal relationship with God, so she worshipped in her own way and didn't require a church to do so. Now, as an adult, I wonder if the fact that my father never went to church, unless we went as a family on a high holy day, had something to do with it. For his part, Dad could hardly reconcile all the gold, silver and marble in churches when people were starving somewhere in the world.

Why am I mentioning spirituality when this book is about money being energy? Because we are divine beings having a human experience, as described in A Course in Miracles (ACIM), and, well, everything is energy; states of consciousness, energy, spirituality… they are pretty much all the same thing in the end. And what we may have been taught about money from well-meaning family members, religious institutions, various communities, educational organizations, etc., during our childhood and early adult years, may not be, in reality, the way it actually is. With all things, we have the power in every conscious moment to choose—to make the choice of decision and what we believe. I'm writing this book so you may choose wisely, and together we raise the money consciousness of the world for prosperity for all.

Ever since I can remember I wore my heart on my sleeve—always cried at the drop of a hat, been too sensitive. And I was forever into boys—co-dependence, anyone? From my first couple of heart throbs at the tender young age of nine (in Guayaquil, Ecuador) and thirteen (back in the States) to the grade school crushes—memorably one who asked me to marry him at sixteen (I said yes, of course, but we ended it a year later)—to marrying my high school sweetheart (we divorced). And then from marrying my "from-another-life heart throb" with two children (we divorced), to, ultimately, my soul mate (we are celebrating eighteen years of marriage and twenty years of partnership at this writing). I have remained an eternal optimist. I have always lived through my heart. No wonder I learned in adulthood that it is the most intelligent of all our energy centers.

Also, as an adult, through Women's Prosperity Network and Nancy Matthews, I was introduced to Wallace D. Wattles' *The Science of Getting Rich*, and discovered how spiritual money really is, and how it is connected to our fullest expression on this planet.

Realizing my money story was similar to my love life, I wrote "My Perfect Storms" in *Courage Under Siege, From Adversity to Victory* in 2017 (which became an international bestseller), to share that we can rise above the negatives in our lives—even financially—and prevail. I always trusted things would work out and worked my way up the corporate ladder, to the best of my ability, *without* a college degree. I didn't have any intentions around money—

growing it, receiving it, or giving it (beyond tithing to my church). That is, until I realized that the energy we express in our bodies has quite a bit to do with how much money does come into, and stay in, our lives.

There is a set point. My realization had been set by the example of my mother, in whose shoes I followed upon graduating from high school. I went to Katharine Gibbs School and achieved an eight-month certification in Secretarial Studies, which allowed me to cut my teeth on Wall Street, at the sweet-starting annual salary of $16,500. (My mom, today, is an executive assistant for the founding partner of a private brokerage firm.) Fast forward four years, to when I moved to the informational side of the financial industry, where I stayed for eight years. That was followed by twelve years on the insurance side of the industry. It was during this time that I had a crisis of *legacy*.

Why do I call it a crisis of legacy? I couldn't see my footprint. I felt I wasn't leaving anything behind of value, of heritage. Even though I had an amazing manager, made a six-figure salary with benefits, had the second half of my college paid for by the company, and had a terrific team, I was no longer fulfilled at a soul level. I knew I was here on this earth for more than this. I followed the guidance of one of my advisors at the time to move to the client-facing side of the industry. I thought I had found my calling! Fast forward eight more years, and I realized **no matter their income, people are unaware how to invite in and receive whatever money they desire, so they can be, do and have more.**

Meanwhile, I was in my current marriage and had accumulated a bunch of debt along the way and via the two divorces beforehand.

It had taken me a while to develop my sense of self-worth as well—but not until paying the ultimate financial price of bankruptcy. My credit cards had gotten way out of hand. The sufficient cash flow from my mid-career change into the client-facing side took a bit longer than anticipated to replace the six-figure corporate salary and lifestyle, of which I had grown accustomed to.

It was during this time when I began hiring coaches so I could quantum-leap, leveraging their hard-won experience, and achieved year *ten* results by year *three*. As a mid-career changer, I had no time to waste in getting my income back to "normal" in an "eat-what-you-kill" arena. In one fell swoop I went from solid corporate soldier to self-employed entrepreneur, and I needed help. Fast.

When you hire coaches, you are able to step on their shoulders and be propelled forward, faster and farther than with trial and error. You also have a knowledgeable resource close at hand for when things don't go as planned or the unexpected turns occur—as they are inclined to do in life.

My fourth coach, Renee Gambino (www.reneegambino.com), who is super innovative and wildly successful herself, helped me figure out some disconnects inside my service process and sales conversation to retain folks in my method through to completion and implementation. My financial practice experienced a 35% year-over-year increase the first year working with Renee. And in my second year of working with her, she was essential in my discovering the seven energetic levels of money consciousness.

Let me tell you how it started.

Renee was doing her magic with me one day and observed, "I suspect that when you do a financial plan for someone, you do more than a financial plan."

I confirmed she was accurate, because I'm all in for my clients. Over the years, I have provided career support, relationship tips, mentored client's children, and so on. Renee further observed, knowing full-well that the biggest opportunity for increasing the money your business provides is to take a serious look at where you are giving away value, that we could turn that value into revenue. There had to be a way. Renee set about to help me identify those talents, skills and services, and we discovered that I had the makings of a coach. Renee, through her Socratic questioning methodology, helped me re-engage with a text I had read previously.

In 2016, one of my sisters gifted me Christie Marie Sheldon's *Love or Above* program, a series of audio tracks designed to expand one's awareness of how to create the life one wants by working with one's energy. She had mentioned Sir David Hawkins's *Power v. Force* book, and I read it that year. In reading it a second time two years later, I figuratively hit my forehead with the heel of my hand and said, "This is exactly how money works!"

Through several rounds of conversation, research and review, Renee helped me refine this signature discovery into the "7 Energetic Levels of Money Consciousness." This occurred in mid-2018, and by that summer, we launched my beta group coaching program, and I became a coach—of course, only after it was approved as an Outside Business Activity (OBA) by my financial firm's compliance team. This is when I discovered my legacy work, as I want to raise the money consciousness of the world for prosperity for all. I may have already mentioned that earlier in this first chapter.

As you can see from the following image, the **7 Money Realities** build from the ground up, expanding and getting lighter as they go up and outward. This is because the energy of money, as it grows, gets bigger and lighter. Hawkins created his "Map of Consciousness" whereby one can measure the energetic vibration of any state of mind, consciousness or energy in the body. His scale is from 0 (Death) to 1,000 (Jesus, Krishna, Buddha), with 900 as the vibration of gratitude, the highest vibrational frequency we humans can embody in the physical realm.

In the next chapter, I describe the **7 Money Realities** and provide guidance on how to move from one level to the next. You will be able to identify where you are in the energetic levels of money consciousness. It all starts with awareness! I should know. It's of no coincidence that in 2019, we had a quantum leap household year of $1 million plus. We moved into the house of our dreams, up-leveled my car, and added a Mediterranean apartment to our lives, among other things. And I can trace it all back to learning in 2016 that energy and vibration and frequency, with intention and self-work, can make everything possible.

7 Money Realities & Realizations™

7. **Enlightened Gratitude**

6. **Joyful Completion**

5. **Loving Money**

4. **Harmonious Acceptance**

3. **Courageous Forgiveness**

2. **Captive Desire**

1. **Deficient Absence**

Chapter Two

The 7 Money Realities™

Having made my signature discovery of the "7 Energetic Levels of Money Consciousness," I was excited to share it with the world! I began with a group of about thirty friends and acquaintances with what was initially conceived as a thirty-day beta program. However, as we journeyed together, they kept asking for more and more information. My initial group program morphed into a ninety-day program!

What happens for us humans, as we seek to move to our next level, regardless of the area of life or business, we meet resistance. The initial resistance is usually our ego mind, that part of us that has an important role to play of keeping us alive to breathe another day. It has a tendency, unless we are equipped with practices and tools to manage it, to perceive threats where none exist and create circumstances that maintain the status quo.

As I ran the beta group, I recognized where this was occurring and built in additional support and materials to avoid any back-sliding while expansion occurred for my clients. Then, I added one-on-one coaching. And results were becoming more and more evident. My clients sold their residences for their asking price or better, for cash, by their established deadline. They acquired next-level clients and income. They improved their career environment. They retired a spouse. They up-leveled their cars, their houses, their families' lives. And there was a noticeable ripple effect within six months after working with me, too. They paid off massive business debt and thrived during COVID-19 months, achieving their best ever income after ten or twenty years in business!

For them, as for you, learning the **7 Money Realities** was their first step in understanding that unlimited opportunities abound all around us all the time, and abundant prosperity is our birthright.

Let's begin.

The 7 Money Realities™ Levels

Life-taking energetic levels of money consciousness include the first and second levels. These levels literally drain away your energy. They make creation a terrific strain, if not impossible most times.

Level 1: Deficient Absence
(Shame, Guilt, Despair, Blame states of mind)

This first level propels ABUNDANCE away from you consistently, there is a feeling of falling into a black hole financially and unable to dig yourself out of that hole because you are disconnected from ABUNDANT PROSPERITY. This shows up in bankruptcy, collections, repossessions, liens, and credit shut down—even homelessness. It is a very precarious, scary, fear-filled, anxious level to be in, and one in which you desire to be out of as quickly as possible.

To move to Level 2, cultivate the desire for more and better, and improvement of your current situation; it's simply a DECISION—energy follows intent—and *then* take action, "5-4-3-2-1" (a la Mel Robbins' rocket launch countdown approach).

Level 2: Captive Desire

(Enslaved craving, Anxiety, Non-Belief states of mind)

This is a noticeable improvement from Level 1 because it attracts UNFULFILLED ATTACHMENT consistently. It is craving a better life financially. Without the faith you can achieve it. You remain a slave to your ego which shows up as reliance on proof rather than belief. If anything changes (you get sick, or need to take a day off), you are "done" and will have to borrow or simply not pay. It is a perilous place to be.

To move to Level 3, cultivate a willingness to try, keep an open mind to trust the Universe & Universal Law. A book I recommend to my clients at this level, if they haven't been previously exposed to Universal Law and its connection to energy, is Deepak Chopra's *The 7 Spiritual Laws of Success,* a great primer on these laws.

You are now at a turning point in the levels. We go from life-taking to life-giving levels! And it starts with courage. The astute reader will observe that Level 3 is not technically in the middle of the seven levels, and that's correct. But because the energy is exponential and grows outward as well as upward, Level 3 becomes the pivotal level that separates life-taking from life-giving experiences.

Level 3: Courageous Forgiveness

(Willingness to accepting responsibility, Release from past mistakes, No blaming, Compassion, Trust in Universe states of mind)

Level 3 intentionally attracts STARTER ABUNDANCE consistently, through conscious practice. It is about gaining objectivity on past mistakes and shows up as listing out all credit owed, becoming and remaining aware of every dollar owed, knowing your expenses to the penny, and taking responsibility and control over results. Important to note: You start to reclaim your inner, innate power at this stage. You have a role to play in all results, and you forgive yourself for past mistakes and are willing to take responsibility for making different decisions going forward. You start taking, and continue to take, each next micro-action to the ABUNDANT PROSPERITY you desire.

To move to Level 4, focus on acceptance, forgiveness, being open to receiving, believing in the sufficiency of the Universe, without concern about the "how." This is achieved through detachment to the outcome while taking your next micro-action for prosperity.

Level 4: Harmonious Acceptance

(Courageous release / Transcendence of attachment to outcome, Non-Judgment states of mind)

Here we consistently attract MEANINGFUL ABUNDANCE and SUFFICIENCY through energetic flow and magnetism. It is about being continually in the flow, open to signs and signals along the way, beginning to appreciate that before you are a thought, you are energy. And when you manage your energy first, and then take action, you have a clear five-year vision and twelve-month plan for your money, you leverage experts in money, you read books on money.

To move to Level 5, cultivate understanding and love, send compassion for all, move into curiosity: "I wonder why…" and see all feedback as positive information that informs your next step. *Pro Tip: Write a love letter to money!*

Level 5: Loving Money
(Embodying love, Compassion states of mind)

In this level one maintains the FLOW OF MONEY and attracts ALIGNED OPPORTUNITIES, feeling at peace with all. Anytime you spend money or pay bills, you bless your checking/banking account and wallet. You love being in the flow of money and attract opportunities to make more money. You treat yourself and loved ones well with your money and are able to say yes to being generous—you are your money. Receiving money feels expansive and it feels so easy and natural to receive it, which opens the door for receiving even more.

To move to Level 6, see the world as one, as in everything is energy and we are all connected. Know that what you do on the personal scale/level affects everyone globally (prosperity for ALL!).

Level 6: Joyful Completion
(Blissful illumination, Serenity states of mind)

Here we attract PROSPERITY & OVERFLOW consistently and with EASE. You have more than enough and keep attracting more, efficiently, and you give back, charitably, on a regular basis.

There is a prevalent feeling of bliss and being a deep, still pond where everything money-wise is positive, buoyant, expansive and plentiful.

To move to Level 7, cultivate and "BE" enlightenment, express gratitude for all things—say, "I am so happy and grateful for [x] and better is on its way!"—including the good/ugly, the big/small, as often as possible.

Level 7: Enlightened Gratitude

(Omnipresence, Ever-present gratefulness / thankfulness)

You have arrived at peak money consciousness, which attracts ABUNDANCE, SUFFICIENCY, PROSPERITY & OVERFLOW, exponentially. Few people attain this level. Your wealth grows exponentially with little effort or focus, while you focus solely on your purpose, knowing exponential wealth springs from it. You may have glimpses of this level and be unable to stay in it. BEing gratitude all the time for all things and being connected to a state of everlasting flow is a requirement to stay in this level.

Enough cannot be said of gratitude. As Wallace D. Wattles says in *The Science of Getting Rich*, "…gratitude brings your whole mind into closer harmony with the creative energies of the universe."

Harmony has flow, and being in a state of gratitude aligns you with the abundant prosperity that is your birthright, and your responsibility.

Wattles also states that "…life, by living, multiplies itself."

It is therefore good and right that you desire all the juicy goodness, all the riches, in store for you. The desire for more life is built within your DNA. Teeming, abundant life is your natural state, which is why it feels so good. And gratitude gets you there. We will explore this at length in the next chapter.

Chapter Three

Moving Toward Ever-Expanding Money Consciousness

I remember the day it clicked for me: The day I realized that the key is being grateful for it all, no matter what. Unless we are grateful for everything, and yes, that means everything, even when the you-know-what is hitting the fan, we are not truly vibing gratitude.

It started out as a disagreement with my husband, and of course, I cannot recall what the issue was. It happened on a weekend, when I had a personal to-do list a mile long and had to leave the house to run my errands, or they would never get done.

As I drove down our long driveway, before I reached the end, I had an epiphany! Here I was, distracted by the unresolved argument, feeling pressure to get all my errands done, feeling pretty low emotionally, and running things over and over in my mind, when, BAM! I proverbially hit my hand to forehead and said, "Oh! I get it! I get to be grateful for even THIS!" It was my turning point in embracing the energy of gratitude.

Have you ever noticed how many people say they are grateful for everything? And then, when you listen closely to what they say and how they say it, there's an underlying current of negativity?

That's because they haven't really gotten the realization (yet) that gratitude for everything and in all things truly means just that. Even the "not so good" stuff.

So here I am in my car, making a left turn, and I get this epiphany. Before I turn onto the road, I take a pause and say out loud that I'm extremely grateful for the disagreement with my husband. And just like that, my energy shifted. It shifted out of pity, frustration, anger, and impatience to expansiveness, forgiveness and joy—that I have a partner with whom to disagree from time to time. That I have a house and life we share. That I had plenty of time, space and energy to take care of my errands.

Fast forward to returning home, I began to put away my purchases. You cannot imagine my surprise when, lo and behold, my husband came down from his upstairs office, found me in the kitchen, and…wait for it…apologized! You could have knocked me over with a feather.

What had happened was, and this is exactly how energy works because it is beyond all time, space and dimension, in being grateful for the disagreement (and everything else), which shifted my energy, it also shifted his energy, even though he wasn't in my immediate presence. Not only that, but in shifting my own energy, I quite literally forgot about the disagreement, and he undoubtedly felt that shift and it created space for him to apologize first.

It does take two to tango, as they say, so of course I apologized for my role in the disagreement as well. And ever since that epiphany, I have been mindful of what can happen when we achieve gratitude at all times (or as much as possible) no matter what the circumstance or situation is.

The main thing to remember is what this means in terms of the **7 Money Realities**. Since gratitude is the highest vibration we humans can hold in the physical body, when we embody it "no matter what," we become a vibrational match to the next level, regardless of in which level we are.

Here is an important side note to this. Since we manifest through our body, because we live on a physical plane and we receive money through the physical, it is essential that we take good care of ourselves. There are several types of self-care that impact how abundantly we can invite in and receive more money.

Physical: This includes sleep, physical activity and release, making healthy food choices, rest and relaxation. For me, I have always been a person who falls asleep the minute her head hits the pillow. And, if I need to have more sleep but am time crunched, I use hypnotic meditation to create it with less time. Did you know that ten minutes of hypnotic meditation is worth two hours of sleep? In terms of making healthy food choices, I start the day with a whole foods supplement and go from there. R&R (rest and relaxation) are what I do on the days of the week I do not work—and here's the thing: I find I attract more juicy goodness when I take time and rest! Fun is also high vibe and quite attractive and generative.

Emotional: This includes stress management, emotional intelligence, forgiveness, compassion, and kindness. Being in, and remaining in, a high-level emotional state also helps magnetize what we want to our lives.

Social: In this category are such things as boundaries, support systems, communication, spending time together, asking for help. As an adult, it is your right and responsibility to communicate your needs and have them answered. Being able to ask for what you want is essential because you receive money through other people when you serve them at your highest level, and you get to ask to serve them.

Spiritual: Here is where the passive meditative practices come in, like yoga and other meditation, spending time alone, journaling, being in sacred space, nature, connection. Reflection and contemplation are the only ways you can review and course-correct. If you don't practice this, you run the risk of never-ending days and not having what you want in the end. When you pause and reflect, you raise your awareness and consciousness to higher realms, connect with insight and intuition, and are able to co-create with the Universe.

If any of these areas are popping up for you as you read them, I would strongly encourage and invite you to consider what would need to be true in order for you to change that area of your life. See what answers come up for you and explore the best way to get started in one of those areas. Feel free to move to another area or section of the same area in a step-by-step fashion, as it's easiest for us humans to change on a bit-by-bit basis.

Pro-Tip: There are two ways to get different results. One is slow and steady over time, and the other, more of a Quantum Leap method, is to give yourself a new experience. I favor the latter. And when I initially started, it was more of a slow and steady type of approach. Use whichever works best for you.

In the **7 Money Realities**, there is a turning point of COURAGE in Level 3. So, remember dear heart, take courage. When your ego mind throws up circumstances in the form of an emergency or a disagreement with a partner or family member, or what have you, take courage. Remember that life is not linear. It is an ever-unfolding dance with the Universe. And with this new knowledge and understanding of the energies at play and how to navigate and engage them, you will want to step into courage and keep expanding upward and outward.

In addition, intention and desire are powerful forces. In fact, Wattles says, "Desire is a manifestation of power." When you do what you most want to do, it leads to the most fulfillment. And a sense of fulfillment registers high on the list of what my clients say they want in life. Because when you are fulfilled, your cup runs over, your bank accounts are filled with surplus and overflow, your prosperity, legacy and generosity are expanded, and you are filled to exploding with life!

The way this translates into inviting in and receiving more money is that money is the effect and service is the cause. Sales (which is asking to be in service to another) is what gets you into service in the first place. If you believe that only people in business are salespeople, please read David Pink's *To Sell is Human*. In fact, all humans sell. Even mothers must "sell" their ideas to their children, such as broccoli is good for you.

When you intend to have more money, and you desire to express your highest-level service in exchange, while being extremely detailed and crystal clear on exactly what money you want and by when, you are in alignment with the fact that the Universe rewards specificity and decisiveness. When you cultivate your energetic vibration higher and higher in an ongoing and consistent manner, you align with attracting higher and higher levels of money and prosperity. You, in essence, become a match for what you want to magnetize and receive.

Since money comes to you through other people, it also stands to reason that the right people will be attracted to you through your energy so that more money will come to you through them when you serve them. The biggest area of improvement I see when people first start to implement these teachings is that they fail to up-level their ideal audience or client. This all goes hand in hand, and it's one of the things I teach my clients. Who are they now serving, what's the new value exchange, so they serve at their highest level while receiving the money they want?

And since I mentioned want, it's important to state here that you always get what you need. You always meet your "need line," as Bob Proctor teaches. The trick, so to speak, is to raise our need line. It is for this reason that I have exercises I give my clients that expand their need line and also their awareness of this new need line.

Remember, everything is energy and so is money. You want to move upwards in an ever-expanding money consciousness, so that you can invite in and receive the money you truly want. This takes leadership, which we explore in the next chapter. How do you lead yourself (and others) when it comes to your money, and why is this important to, well, everything? You start with being in gratitude for everything at all times, beginning with being in gratitude as often as possible, at first. You add on taking care of yourself, so you can actually, physically, magnetize and manifest what you want in your life. And you get clear on exactly what that is, what money you want, and what you agree and commit to give in exchange for it.

Next up is the importance of leadership, starting with self-leadership.

Chapter Four

Leading Your Money, Which Touches Everything

There is much out in the world about leadership. Leading others, leading oneself, and the like. Little time is devoted to talking about leading one's money, or why it's so essential. Consider that, first and foremost, everything is energy, including money. So, as we've been saying, inviting in and receiving your birthright of abundant prosperity (unapologetically, no less) is all about the energetics of it. Additionally, YOU direct your energy; in fact, you lead it with your intention.

People naturally desire to follow a good leader. And so does money. Good leaders lead by example. They also give credit where credit is due and acknowledge teamwork. We co-create with the Universe/God/Spirit (however you conceive this Entity/Force). Wallace D. Wattles calls it Intelligent Substance, that is waiting for you to impress your thought upon it, so IT can bring it about. You must impress your free will in choosing what you want, ensuring you are an energetic match to it, and working within Universal Law to invite it in and receive it. The action in the physical is asking for what you want. You lead your money by honoring it, being a good steward of it, and knowing what good works you will do with it when it arrives in surplus and overflow, because you asked for it for a purpose. Good leaders know how to ask for the desired outcome, from themselves, their teams and their money.

My ability to lead my money shifted over time; the more I learned and understood about standing on a wall for principles (and my clients) and what my non-negotiable values are (and they do evolve, by the way), the more I realized the requirement of leading my money.

Rather than be subject to the middle-class mindset, where circumstances are energized over Truth, you want to lead your money from your next level mindset—which is an abundance and prosperity mindset—by energizing Truth over circumstance, believing that life happens FOR you, and gaining clarity on your non-negotiables.

For example, when I decided that being a multi-million-dollar entrepreneur was non-negotiable for me, and I worked with my multiple coaches in my two businesses on that strategy, as well as energized more money and windfalls in our personal lives together with my husband, everything shifted. From an energy-forward place, I claimed what I wanted, released myself from however it was going to show up and acted as if it was a reality. In 2019, we enjoyed a more than million-dollar household year.

In 2020, when the global pandemic hit the U.S. in the first quarter and continued to affect society and business through the third quarter (where and when this book is being written), it was the great amplifier. If you had a solid financial plan, it amplified that. If you had a solid abundance and prosperity mindset, it amplified that. If you didn't, it amplified that.

Because I had a solid routine of my daily practice, opening my heart center, setting my energy ball of intention for the day, writing gratitude statements and what I call, "Reality Statements," where I claim the money I desire by the desired date because prosperity enables me to relax and so be healthier, while releasing from the how (and how it will show up), I attracted money other than through my two businesses, as well as through one of my businesses which was "essential." And in this quarter, into the fourth quarter, I am positioned to still make my annual revenue goal of $1.5 million.

Leaders never quit and quitters never lead (which is a turn on a well-known saying)! There is an external way to lead which is more masculine, there is an internal way to lead which is more feminine, and then there is an integrated way to lead, and lead your money, which is the next level. It's all in; all parts of you working in conjunction with the Universe to bring about what you desire in a way that serves your highest and greatest good. And what's in your highest and greatest good is in everyone else's highest and greatest good.

Renee Gambino taught me many invaluable lessons as my business strategist for multiple years, and the one that's most applicable here is that leading yourself at your next and highest level entails embracing and implementing the idea that you must value yourself and others *equally*. Until and unless that occurs, you are not leading yourself or your money as optimally as possible. Remember, money is the EFFECT; service to others is the CAUSE. And when you value everyone in that exchange equally, the money flow occurs with ease, grace and natural abundance.

Just the other day, a prospect of mine, in the midst of his decision-making process about whether he was willing to invest in himself to have the money results he desires, attempted to negotiate the investment level down by about 17%. Because I know the value of the results he will enjoy from working together, I held the line and led him successfully to fully appreciate why the investment was what it was, why waiting the four months he initially expressed would cost him tens of thousands of dollars by not implementing what I teach, to ultimately choose to proceed. He said yes to himself, and I was so happy and grateful to inspire him through standing on a wall for Truth over circumstance and leading with integrity and for his non-negotiable success.

Belief shapes reality. When we shift those beliefs, and shift them permanently, our reality changes. In my programs, private and group alike, one of the core things we work through are your money beliefs. Many clients say this is the major shift they receive through working with me. Some are even shocked to realize that, at their advanced age, they were never consciously aware of what they were taught, and subsequently believe and still believe, about money. They are gratified to be taught they have choice; they have power over what they believe. As a child, you did not have the tools to discern for yourself of what to believe. So you accept without question everything that is taught to you, up until about age seven. By that point, your programming is so set you do not recognize you have any choice. Therefore, you proceed along as programmed.

If, as an example, your parents never talked about money, you yourself don't talk about money—not with yourself and certainly not with others. Or perhaps your parents were polar opposites.

One saved money, perhaps even hoarded it, fearful it wouldn't last or one day would run out altogether, and the other spent it gleefully, without so much as a care in the world. Whichever the case, know that your current beliefs about money, especially if they are no longer serving you (i.e., they are based in a lack mindset), can be acknowledged and shifted to whatever you choose to think about money.

Because in the end, you truly don't want the money itself, the paper and coin. You want what the money enables you to be, do and have. That's the true currency and energy of money. Here is a suggestion. Think about how you want to feel about money. If you could feel about money in any way you wanted, what would that be? Once you arrive at that, translate that desired feeling to a belief about money. For example, if you want to feel that receiving lots of money is expansive, easy and fun, then you can choose a new belief about money that, instead of rich people being greedy, or rich people being all about the money (as many have told me they believe before we shift those beliefs), money is a good, beneficial and abundant substance.

I recently had a client ask me how "acting as if" works. This is often misunderstood. She believed that to be abundant she needed to act abundantly up front and spend lots of money, and it would return to her in kind. The truth is, we must "act as if" in our energy first, which will bring the money to us easier, and then "act as if" in our physical actions on the physical plane. It's sort of like trying to be charitable from an empty bank account. It doesn't work. What does work is leading energy forward and acting as if you already have the essence of what the money will give you, serving the heck out of your ideal clientele from your highest level (whether in business or career), receiving the commensurate money, and then you'll be abundant.

You see, the reality is ... prosperity is a good thing. The more prosperous you are, the more generous you become, and also, the more healthy you become—because prosperity enables you to relax and be healthier—which only improves your ability to attract and create more prosperity, and so on. The more prosperous your family is, the more you can help others, help your community, help your nation, help your world. And so on and so on.

And the great news is that the energy of money and prosperity is a catchy thing. When you lead it from your energy—because energy is exponential and exists beyond all space, time and dimension—you can uplift others in your community simply by being your most prosperous self.

When we moved to our new home in a very rural setting in a different state, we were shocked at how poor the roads were. I mean, there were multiple craters in the seventeen miles we drove to our nearest town! We researched the timing of when the Department of Transportation were planning a resurfacing, only to be disappointed to hear it was about two to three years away from reaching our area! Undeterred by this "reality," every time I was driving on our local roads, I would imagine them smooth and new. Within six months, the trees along the sides were trimmed, drainage ditches re-dug, and holes were filled and patched, with marked improvement. Within another two months, they were resurfaced and repaved. Driving on our roads is such a pleasure now that our dairy farmer neighbor shared her delight about driving to town on the new roads. That good-will feeling of all the drivers on our roads, including visitors from out of state, will only serve to fuel more good will. The feeling of, and experience of, prosperity is a catchy thing.

Another important aspect of money leadership is taking 100% responsibility for your results. This means taking ownership of the role you play. Remember you are co-creating with the Universe, leading with your free will. The Universe is a willing partner, supporting your every move. And you've got to make the first one. Stepping fully into the role of initiator means determining your money goal and by when you want it. Then being an energetic match to that level of money, remaining open to the how, and once receiving the how, taking aligned action every day toward that money goal. As another mentor likes to say, it is 90% energy and 10% implementation.

Most people do it the other way around. They focus on all the effort. They believe they must work harder and longer to attain greater money results. I am here to tell you it is actually so much easier than that. In fact, once we are open to considering there is another (easier) way, the way typically appears. Because now we have a different, more expanded perspective on things. We see a wider horizon, more options, things we didn't previously perceive. It's practically a new world. And we ourselves are not the same people we were before when we had our previous perspective.

As I learned from Renee, as we do one thing, we do everything. And as I learned from another mentor, until we don't. This means we are on an ever-evolving path or journey. Just as the cells in our body regenerate on the physical level, our consciousness is ever evolving. Which is why whenever I start working with people, either individually or in a group setting, I invite them to empty their cup and open their minds to hearing what it is being shared as if they never heard it before.

First, you can practically never hear good things often enough (thus, repeated readings of the same scripture in a church). Second, leading your money touches everything else. It enables you to apply that leadership to other areas of life, as well as enjoy the prosperity you desire to expand your generosity and your legacy. It feeds your soul and enables you to feed the souls of others along the way. Because that's how energy works. Raise yourself and you inspire others to follow suit—as I trust I have been doing for you throughout this book.

Chapter Five

The Spiritual Side of Money Consciousness (It's a Blessing)

Believe it or not, you have everything, every resource, every piece of wisdom and knowledge, every ounce of energy and more...all within you already! You just forgot. In the living of life, pursuing a career or launching a business, learning the how of all of that, perhaps starting a family, and evolving over the journey of life, it all can tend to become unconscious standard. You can somehow slip into the routine of going through the motions or becoming so distracted by a current goal and what you have in front of your face that you lose sight of the source of it all.

Source is source. And you are connected to Source (AKA God, Intelligent Substance, the All-Knowing, the Universe, etc.), at all times. To feel that connection, you must be aware of it. You must remember that it's always there, and through that connection, you get to co-create, you get to impress upon that Entity everything you want—your dreams and aspirations, your intentions, and your willingness to receive it all—and more! You get to have it any way you want.

This is such a blessing! In keeping with the Truth that everything is energy, and so is money, when you bless something or someone, which is what I do as I drive in my car, you not only increase their energy, you increase yours. And in that mutual expansion, it becomes exponential. According to Christie Marie Sheldon, who plays with energy for a living and helps her clients get their life to look a certain way, explains that the energy of a blessing, or the action of blessing someone or something (like your wallet), registers high on the energetic frequency scale. It simply makes sense to do this often.

You may already be familiar with Dr. Thurman Fleet's 1934 founding of Concept Therapy, in which THOUGHTS create your FEELINGS, which in turn direct your ACTIONS, which then deliver your RESULTS. Good news! Thoughts are the *gateway* to your ENERGY, or your embodiment of energetic frequency.

Follow me here. In every conscious moment, you have the power of choice. This means, you can *choose* what energetic frequency you embody in every moment. The way you experience life to be however you desire it to be is within your grasp. And if you are, indeed, energy before you are a thought, then the highest level frequency you can BE in your human body, the more powerful your thoughts will be, influencing your Feelings to be of the highest states of consciousness, which means your actions will be aligned and your results a given. When you are in this highest level of yourself, you cannot fail!

Albert Einstein is known for saying, "Everything is energy and that's all there is to it. Match the frequency of the reality you want and you cannot help but get that reality. It can be no other way. This is not philosophy. This is physics." It is based in scientific and Universal Law.

And look, we don't want money. We want what the money gets us or does for us, so we can do, be, and have more. Like taking better care of ourselves, our family, our community. Or giving back more. The more money we have, the better options we have, the more secure we feel, the higher confidence we have in our future, the more fulfilled we are, and the more fully expressed we become. In fact, in *The Science of Getting Rich*, Wallace D. Wattles states that desiring money for what it can get us or do for us is noble. There is no higher pursuit.

Remember, in the **7th Money Reality** of "Enlightened Gratitude," the energy frequency match one must be is light and expansive, and in that level, we don't even focus on the money, but solely on our highest purpose in life and its pursuit. Money becomes an effortless after effect. It is guaranteed to be plentiful, abundant and without limit. What a noble pursuit, indeed!

As I said, money consciousness is a blessing, which is super high energy. It is a blessing to the world when you pursue your highest expression of yourself, because it serves humankind at its highest and greater good. And because money is the EFFECT, and service is the CAUSE, the more you are, and choose to be, at CAUSE, the greater your impact and the larger is the EFFECT you receive in kind. What a win-win!

I will contend that to break through to being consciously in choice as often as possible, until you are in that state 24/7, takes some discipline, some training of sorts. What I have found most useful personally—and I share it here with you to help you on your own prosperity journey—is having a daily routine. It is most powerful when you prioritize this activity before all others. In my day, when

I wake and the coffee is being made, I light a candle, saying "I am awake, I'm present, and I am powerful." (Thank you, Elizabeth Purvis.) This gives a clear and unmistakable signal to my brain that we are starting our Daily Practice. I have a methodology for this that I teach my clients, which they can make their own along the way.

What, in essence, this ritual does for me is, first and foremost, connect me with my spiritual or Divine side, and from there express gratitude by journaling three things I'm grateful for. And then I write what I call my "Reality Statements," expressing what I desire in money as if it already happened.

Because where you focus, you manifest. Engaging a prosperity practice will do just that—bring you more prosperity. It will open you up with gratitude for everything you already have and everything that is on its way. It will seed the expectation that your life, person, experiences, and yes, money, are all enriched. This is your natural birthright, remember. It is in your DNA to be totally and completely healthy, loved, supported, and abundantly rich. Just by breathing, you are worthy of it all.

It is truly "just" a decision. That's not to minimize it. It is a decision, using your conscious power in every moment, of where to direct your focus, your attention, your energy. Once made, the decision has power behind it to bring your desires into being, which I call "realize," or to make real. We can decide to be sad or happy, depressed or inspired, empty or full. In the spiritual realm where all is possible, where there is pure potentiality and anything can happen, you are invited to co-create with that magnificent Source of it all. In fact, Source wants you to have what you want even more than you want to have it!

In your daily ritual, you have the opportunity to reconnect with your true and highest self, the part of you that is Divine. This, as your set-point going forward, maintains your expanded consciousness, your perception, and engagement of your higher level faculties. In this expanded state, it is already accomplished that you should engage your highest-level skillset and talents in the service to humanity…and be paid handsomely in return. Everything is an energy exchange. It is truly a blessing to all, including you!

In fact, we are all one. I have a gift from a long-ago friend hanging on my office wall that says: "Namaste. I honor the place in you in which the entire universe dwells. I honor the place in you which is of love, of truth, of light, and of peace. When you are in that place in you, and I am I that place in me, We are one."

Truly. And this applies to what's in our highest and greater good. In that "we are one" space or dimension, whatever is in my highest and greater good, because we are one, must indeed be in your (and everyone else's) highest and greatest good. It's not selfish, it's selfless. It's being in full service to "we are one" and in that full service, showing up as your highest self-expression of your unique skills and talents (that no one on the face of the Earth has ever, does, or ever will, have in the same combination), that unlocks the abundant prosperity exchange in return. In other words, when are abundantly ourselves, fully expressed, we can open up our arms wide and receive the bounty that cannot fail to be received in return. And so it goes, around and around.

I was reminded in a recent conversation with a young person that none of us are broken. There is nothing to be fixed. We are whole, we are loved, and we each have a purpose. We have a responsibility to each other to live up to our purpose. To serve humanity for the greater good. That's why it feels so right, so good, when we step into that version of ourselves, which is vibrating at our highest level, has full access to our higher level faculties and engages them in service to the greater good. It's what we're built for and what we're here to do, after all.

I invite you to explore energetic frequency and spirituality, if you haven't already. Connecting to a power greater than yourself, and elevating your energy from that place of all-knowingness, pure potentiality, all-seeingness, and all-beingness expands you to the capabilities you are here to fulfill. When I teach my clients about how to best manage their money flow (which is the effect of the cause—service at one's highest level), the first order of business, or the first place their first dollar is allocated to go, is to charitable giving because doing so honors the source of all prosperity, which is Source. When we tithe, which is from agricultural practice of putting a tenth of one's bounty or harvest aside, we are paying homage in thanks to the place from which all comes.

In the next chapter, we will expand on the concept that we are all one and explore why prosperity for all is the ultimate goal for society. It is said that a rising tide raises all ships. In energetic terms, it's an exponential effect. One person with a higher energetic frequency (and therefore enhanced prosperity) can raise up a whole community to vibe higher itself, thereby creating a ripple effect of prosperity.

Chapter Six

Prosperity for All

Let's explore and expand upon the concept that a rising tide raises all ships, and keep in mind that, in energetic terms, this means an exponential effect. Because energy is beyond all time, space and dimension, it adheres not to linear experience. It is beyond it. Therefore, Christie Marie Sheldon is correct in her observation that someone embodying love or above, at a frequency of 500+, can positively impact and uplift the frequencies of 750 other humans on the planet!

Think about that for a hot minute. Imagine the implications. As I said recently to a client, who has a mother-in-law with health issues in another state and a best friend in another, who was saying there's nothing she could do, there is always something we can do for others. The pathway is in the higher levels of dimensionality, in the space of pure potentiality. With energy, there is always something we can do to help others. We can hold space energetically for them.

Let's take a closer look.

First things first. Remember that by breathing, you (and everybody else) are worthy of abundant prosperity in all ways. Riches beyond your imagination. Limitless wealth, health, relationships, plentitude and more. It is your birthright. So as long as you have breath in your body and are willing to open your arms and mind wide open to receive it all, it's yours.

Within this paradigm of anything is possible, and that you are deserving of it already, that means so everyone else is deserving. And if that's true, and we all have a spark of divinity within us, along with the ability to co-create with the Universe and bring about that which we desire, we can all help each other do just that. I put in my daily energy ball, with full on intentionality, that anyone who thinks of me, or is with me, gets love, light, peace, joy and gratitude from me. It's no wonder that people are attracted to my energy when I walk into a room or show up on a virtual gathering.

Whenever I hear people asking for prayer, even if I do not know them (these petitions are prevalent on social media platforms), I take a moment and send them prayer, blessings, and hold space for their perfect health (or whatever the situation calls for—sometimes it's for a missing person or child). Whenever I see posts or shares about unpreferred situations or circumstances, I send blessings and energies of peace and easeful resolution.

This does several things. First, it does actually help the person energetically. Remember, one can affect others energetically, and the intention is to do it for the person's highest and greatest good. In fact, what's in your highest and greatest good is in everyone's highest and greatest good. And vice versa, so it's a win-win all around! Second, people who understand the power of prayer and energy appreciate your help and action on their behalf. It makes them feel listened to, one of our greatest needs, and supported as well. Third, it uplifts not only them and you, but anyone connected to the both of you...up to 750 people total! That's a huge impact from a seemingly "small" thing.

The reason prosperity in all its forms feels so good is that it is our natural state. It is as natural as breathing, walking, talking, being, etc. We tend to lose sight of this in all the busy-ness (business) of living our lives, which takes a lot of doing in the physical realm. One client recently asked me why she couldn't just *be* in the 5-D world and transmit her invitations to work with her from there. I responded that it requires integration with the 3-D and 4-D realms in order to manifest or make real (which I like to call *REALIZE*).

Being in 5-D, great as it is, is disconnected from our earthly world. And it is in and on the physical plane that you must receive the money in exchange for serving up your highest value to the world. So, if you don't integrate and flow between dimensionalities, then you are not effectively serving the world as you are meant to, as you are built to, as you are destined to. And that means, you are not enjoying the abundant prosperity that is your birthright. My client realized where she wasn't serving because of that disconnect, and she stepped into full willingness to say yes to full integration.

In speaking with a young son of a friend recently, who was pretty depressed during 2020's pandemic lock downs and not being able to return to college semester except through online classrooms, we worked through shifting his lower states of consciousness and emotions through hypnosis. My all-time-favorite hypnotist who helped me personally is Dr. Yvonne Oswald, and her book, *Every Word Has Power; Switch on Your Language and Turn on Your Life*, has some awesome exercises to help you resolve any dense or lower vibrational energy.

Once we did that, he was able to think about his highest-level service to the world (and therefore, to himself). He started dreaming a bit again, going back to what he likes, what brings him joy, what gets and keeps him in the zone. The guy is pretty intelligent and leans toward engineering, and when we freed up his energy to go higher and higher, he realized there are unlimited opportunities out there for him, that he had other choices he hadn't been seeing before. A shift of perspective and energy was immensely helpful to him. And, when he expresses that out in the world, he will be the embodiment of his highest and greatest good, which will be in everyone's.

That brings us to my purpose and highest and greatest good. I want to be known for raising the money consciousness of the world for prosperity for all. Two years into my coaching practice about this topic, here I am writing this book, so the ideas and concepts it contains can be more accessible to more people sooner. I humanize the fastest path to inviting in and receiving more money so you can expand your prosperity, generosity and legacy. This is my highest self-expression at this time in history.

And this brings us to an important point. It requires you do you first. That means that, as much as you will want to share these concepts and shout them from the rooftops, so to speak, you must apply them to your life first and foremost. When you do that, you will show people through your embodiment of these principles what is possible, and they will want what you have. That is what I did. In 2019, we had a very bountiful household year. I credit the energy work I did, as a product of my process. I did me first, and the rest followed within a short timeframe.

I want to encourage you to do the same. Focus on your energy. Shifting that will have exponential impact to those around you, your family, your community, your state. Shortly after moving, our roads were repaved. The cynical will say it's because it was an election year. I believe I helped get our rural community roads the attention they deserved by envisioning them repaved any time I drove on them. The original estimates had the road work more than a year out, and we have nice new roads now, over a year sooner than projected.

In the next chapter, I have some suggestions on next steps to engage and receive the level of prosperity you truly desire while serving humanity at your highest level. It does take service because money comes to us through other people. If you think you can have what you want by sitting high on a mountain with no engagement with other people, I would ask you to explore how that serves humanity. The more we serve the humans—and I do love serving the willing humans—the more we receive in kind. It is that simple, really.

In the back of this book there are expansion questions for each chapter, and there is a bibliography to encourage further reading. Life is a never-ending journey, until one day, it is guaranteed to end. Poof! The question is, in that moment, what do you want to be known for? How do you want to be remembered? What legacy do you wish to give to humanity? How could you help others even after you depart this physical plane? In my financial practice, I help people make the best possible financial plan, designed to help them have living benefits and leave something behind to those they love and charitable concerns if they desire.

It is something to think about. There is always a beneficiary if one widens one's perspective, isn't there?

But for now, let us explore the ways to engage and receive that level of prosperity you desire.

Chapter Seven

Where to Go from Here

You now know my story, how I leveraged coaches to assist me in arriving at my signature discovery, what the "7 Energetic Levels of Money Consciousness" are, and ways you can lead your energy and money to be, do and have more. We explored the spiritual side of the equation, as well as the importance of the concept of: What I want for myself, I want for everybody.

We have covered why prosperity for all is a good thing. And when you do you first, all else follows. It is the way energy works. Someone vibrating at 500 or above can positively uplift 750 other souls. Talk about an exponential ripple effect!

To complete your understanding, we now explore where you can go from here and the principles of exponential earning (and living). As mentioned previously, included are additional resources I encourage and invite you to explore, so you continue your learning as you continuously expand your own prosperity, surpassing prior upper limits, and embrace the continual evolution of yourself.

One concept that is key to remember is that you are not the same person as you were even just a moment ago, let alone a year ago, or five years or ten years ago. So, you will not remain the same person you are in this moment. From that perspective, I invite you to consider that every process of growth is designed to be rinsed and repeated or re-applied for ongoing and consistent results.

Sure, you can assess and course-correct along the way. The idea here to embrace is that, similar to emptying your cup when approaching material you may have already been exposed to, the process of moving to your next **Money Reality** level can be repeated and repeated because there is always a new level, or a new dimension of a level. In fact, here is a radical concept. Within each level reside the other levels. So, to move to the next one, you must go through all the levels that are represented within that current level, and then you'll get to the next one, and so forth.

What I'm highlighting here is that the only constant is change. And when you embrace that change, rather than resist it, it becomes your ally in attaining what you want. In money terms, this means that a breakthrough this year becomes the norm and then there is another breakthrough level to attain. Otherwise, you stagnate, and you are not designed to stagnate. You are designed to desire a better tomorrow than today. Notice I'm not talking about being grateful for where you are and then staying right there. I'm talking about being grateful for it all and desiring more. It's not selfish. It's in full-on service to humanity, which needs your particular brand of brilliance.

For example, if money makes everything in life possible, it enables you to fulfill the three reasons for living. As Wallace D. Wattles says in *The Science of Getting Rich*:

"It is perfectly right that you should desire to be rich;…for it is the noblest and most necessary of all studies…for you can render God and humanity no greater service than to make the most of yourself."

He states that man and woman live for three things:

- The body – requiring sustenance, clothing and shelter and time freedom.
- The mind – requiring knowledge and study.
- The soul – requiring love.

These three are denied expression by lack of riches. Therefore, you cannot live up to your fullest potential, and express that potential, without money. And if that's true, and two years ago, I didn't do the work, make my signature discovery, and now write about it in this book, then think of what I would have been denying in terms of service to humanity. Not only did I heal my own money hang-ups, but I get to help others heal theirs.

There is a ripple effect of raising the money consciousness of the world that wouldn't have been expressed if I had chosen to say no to the invitation to go to my next level. In fact, now there is that same invitation, and I get to rinse and repeat, so to speak, the process of saying yes, getting and following guidance by taking daily aligned action, and in full faith, seeing with wonder where it all leads. The Universe wants us to have what we want even more than we want it. Because inherent in the Universal Laws are the impression of increase.

And that brings me to my next point. As I've said, in every conscious moment, you have choice. I have learned it serves me best, and all of humanity, when I consciously choose progress over perfection. One of my earliest mentors was fond of saying (over and over, LOL): "You don't gotta get it right, you just gotta get it going."

Perfection is a dream, an impossibility to attain, so striving for it only sets you up for failure. I prefer to set myself up for success, thank you very much. Action changes everything (otherwise, as Renee likes to say, it all remains a hope or a dream). And choosing progress over perfection allows for action, taking the next micro-action, and knowing you don't need to see the entire plan at one glance. You get to proceed by knowing simply the very next step to move in the right direction toward the highest-level service that causes the highest-level money, ongoing and consistently by rinsing and repeating the process over and over.

One of my favorite Universal Laws is what Deepak Chopra calls "The Law of Pure Potentiality." This is where unlimited opportunities exist, where anything is truly possible. In fact, another mentor of mine likes to say you get to energize Truth over circumstances. What this means is that the Truth is that there are unlimited opportunities, and if you are instead energizing circumstances (what your five senses show you in the moment), you will not be able to see that the money is, in fact, here now. The people you wish to serve at your highest level are, indeed, in your world or your field right now. You are just not seeing the Truth. In order to energize Truth over circumstances, you must be willing to release your addiction to, and reliance upon, your five senses and the 3-D world, and get into your higher-level faculties to leverage your perception, imagination (ability to visualize), memory, intuition, free will (focus), and reason. This will enable you to energize Truth, because you will be able to perceive it through those faculties. Truth cannot be seen, heard, tasted, touched, nor smelled. So, take courage to release yourself from your physical senses in order to leverage the faculties that will serve your next and highest level. And as I like to say, I have courage by the boat load, so if you need some, feel free to borrow mine.

Experts are masters at repeating themselves. Renee Gambino dropped that gem into my brain. To attain mastery requires repeating the fundamentals. I can't tell you how many people drop their enthusiasm when the new becomes the old, when their consistent, ongoing and repeatable results resided in their acceptance of what it takes to attain mastery. As an example, even after many years, I am devoted to my Daily Practice ritual. I allow myself some flexibility, so as to choose progress over perfection. And I know it is the reason my energy and connection to Source remains at the level it is, which drives my ongoing results.

The other mastery concept is to reapply the process in the new level. It works for forever, as long as you rinse and repeat it. As an example, I remember a year ago when I got to up-level my ideal clientele. It was back to the drawing board to go through all the discovery of what their attributes are, what their pain points are, what they want instead and ensuring my language in all my messaging was a match to this new level of whom I was serving. This was a repetitive task for sure, and it got me my next level of people to serve and at higher and higher levels, leading to more money and for longer containers and commitments. I'm applying the very same process to my new ongoing program, so that my clients have support in attaining mastery with money energy and ongoing success.

If you are ready to take action, I invite you to schedule an Expansion Call with me, so you get clarity on what's possible for your money. If I can help you further, I will let you know. If not, I may offer further resources. Remember, there is nothing as generative as clarity.

Book that time with me at:

https://susanglusica.com/schedule/

It is your choice. May you choose wisely and well, my dear reader.

Holding BIG space for your **UNAPOLOGETIC PROSPERITY**!

~ Susan

Expansion Questions

I'm all about teaching and experiencing what works. It is accepted that the physical action of writing with pen in hand formulates new pathways in the brain. It is in the spirit of connection with this innate ability to reprogram oneself through this physical action that I invite you to actively participate in the following Expansion Questions and write (not type or keyboard) your responses. This will more quickly enable you to internalize what you've learned, as well as provide witness to where you will lead your money energy!

Let's begin.

Note: A printable companion guide for these questions is available at:

https://susanglusica.com/MEM-ExpansionGuide/

Chapter One Expansion Question
How I Discovered the 7 Money Realities

Now that you are aware of the spiritual and energetic quality of money, what are your intentions around money for your future?

_____

_____

_____

_____

_____

_____

_____

_____

_____

_____

_____

_____

_____

_____

_____

_____

_____

_____

Chapter Two Expansion Question
The 7 Money Realities

Identify which Money Reality you are currently in and check in with yourself to see whether you desire moving to the subsequent one. If so, are you willing to apply the prescription to move to the next Level? (If so, take action NOW.)

_____

_____

_____

_____

_____

_____

_____

_____

_____

_____

_____

_____

_____

_____

_____

_____

_____

Chapter Three Expansion Question
Moving Toward Ever-Expanding Money Consciousness

What self-care items popped for you and which one are you willing to engage immediately, so you can physically receive more money and abundance?

_____

_____

_____

_____

_____

_____

_____

_____

_____

_____

_____

_____

_____

_____

_____

_____

_____

Chapter Four Expansion Question
Leading Your Money, Which Touches Everything

What are your non-negotiable values? Getting clarity on them will help you lead your money energy, and have ripple effects to other areas of your life. Make a list of your top 10 values, then ask: Is #1 more important to me than #2, etc., until you have your top 3. Those are your top 3 non-negotiables, from which to lead your money.

_____

_____

_____

_____

_____

_____

_____

_____

_____

_____

_____

_____

_____

_____

Chapter Five Expansion Question

The Spiritual Side of Money Consciousness
(It's a Blessing)

In order to plug you into a higher vibrational state now, are you willing to send out blessings to: your family, your wallet, your mailbox/slot, your community, your friends…wherever you may called to send blessings out to? If so, over the next few days, be on the lookout as to how those blessings come back to you in some way, shape or form.

_____

_____

_____

_____

_____

_____

_____

_____

_____

_____

_____

_____

_____

_____

Chapter Six Expansion Question
Prosperity for All

In the spirit of your doing *you first,* ask yourself: "What would it take for me to be prosperous? What would need to be true?" Write down whatever comes in answer. Observe your reaction or response to the answers. Identify what you are willing to change in order to have more prosperity in your life. Make the change now.

_____

_____

_____

_____

_____

_____

_____

_____

_____

_____

_____

_____

_____

_____

_____

Chapter Seven Expansion Question
Where to Go from Here

What is your very next micro-action to inviting in and receiving more money?

It could be an Expansion Call with me!

Take the action NOW and book your appointment here, https://susanglusica.com/schedule/, and I'll look very much to helping you in any way I can!

_____

_____

_____

_____

_____

_____

_____

_____

_____

_____

_____

_____

_____

_____

BONUS Expansion Question

Outcome

What is your Desired Outcome for your money, or Money Reality Level, or Money Reality Desire? And, *by when* do you desire it?

Consider this as you look ahead to the future money experience and relationship with money you are creating: If you could have any level of money, what would that be? If you could create any level of money result for your family (versus for yourself), does it increase or decrease it? And to what do you attribute that effect?

_____

_____

_____

_____

_____

_____

_____

_____

_____

_____

_____

_____

_____

_____

BONUS Expansion Question

Essence

What is the Essence of your Desired Money Outcome/Money Reality Desire? In other words, what does the money enable you to be, do or have? Does it give you security? Confidence? Expansion? Charitable support to others?

_____

_____

_____

_____

_____

_____

_____

_____

_____

_____

_____

_____

_____

_____

BONUS Expansion Question

Expression

What do you believe is your highest level of expression at this time out in the world? If you could innovate or create something new, or re-create/improve on something already in existence, what might that be?

Does this thought progression give you insight into what you might possibly offer out in the world in exchange for the money you desire? How quickly are you willing to take action to invite in and receive it?

_____

_____

_____

_____

_____

_____

_____

_____

_____

_____

_____

_____

ADDITIONAL NOTES

For Further Expansion

Chopra, Deepak. *The Seven Spiritual Laws of Success: A Practical Guide to the Fulfillment of Your Dreams.* Based on Creating Affluence. (San Rafael: Amber-Allen Publishing, 1994).

Hawkins, M.D., Ph.D., Sir David R. *Power vs Force: The Hidden Determinants of Human Behavior.* Author's Official Revised/ Authoritative Edition: An Anatomy of Consciousness. (Carlsbad: Hay House Inc., 1995, 1998, 2004, 2012, 2013).

Matthews, Nancy. "Receiving Your Riches" Course: www.nancymatthews.com/science *based on Wattles' book.

Oswald, Ph.D., MHT, MNLP, MTLTTM, Yvonne. *Every Word Has Power: Switch on Your Language and Turn on Your Life.* (New York: Atria Books/Portland: Beyond Words, 2008).

Pink, Daniel H. *To Sell is Human: The Surprising Truth About Moving Others.* (New York: Riverhead Books, 2013).

Wattles, Wallace D. *The Science of Getting Rich.* (Holyoke: Elizabeth Towne, 1910).

Acknowledgments

As I express to my clients, when you engage mentors, coaches and proper life and business support in your life, you are able to stand on their shoulders and reach farther than you would have without them.

I have had many, spanning across my years as a hungry student (and sponge), in my 20-year corporate career and now in my entrepreneurial endeavors. They are too many to name, and my gratitude to each and every one is unending.

Of note, thanks to Mom and Dad for being my first mentors in life.

Gratitude to Mrs. Mangenelli, who rounded out my rough edges and taught me how to leave Kindergarten with my head held high.

Thanks to David M. Darst for teaching me that straight edges matter.

Hugs to Dr. Rutigliano at NYU for first teaching me how to embody a concept like love (in whose class I met my soulmate).

Joe Sciabica, I'm indebted to you for seeing potential in me that I didn't know was there and introducing me to my first successful entrepreneurial opportunity, which is still rocking!

Thank you to Robert Ball, who taught me true exponential-wealth building.

Thank you to my sales assistant, Lelia Mander, for staying true to our joint mission.

So much appreciation to Nancy Matthews, Trish Carr and Susan Wiener, co-founders of Women's Prosperity Network, where I was introduced to Wallace D. Wattles and Dr. Yvonne Oswald.

To Dr. Yvonne Oswald, whose 2018 hypnotic NLP session was a true turning point, unlocking unlimited potential for me.

Special thanks to the most recent ones at the time this is written who have made my evolution possible by expanding my mind and energy patterns, always encouraged me to see bigger, and held space for what was possible that I could step into:

Renee Gambino, who taught me conscious connection and helped me become aware of my signature discovery.

Elizabeth Purvis, who invited me to play with her in manifesting big money and beyond.

Peggy Lee Hanson, who gave me my first international best-selling authorship opportunity and mid-wifed this book by gently coaching me through the creation process.

Katrina Sawa, who is my innovative marketing coach and gave me my second international best-selling authorship.

Danielle Hoffman, who has unveiled unforeseen dimensions for me to play even bigger than ever.

It's a blessing to play with all of you!

May you be blessed with mentors, coaches and support in your life and business/career, as I have been!

About the Author

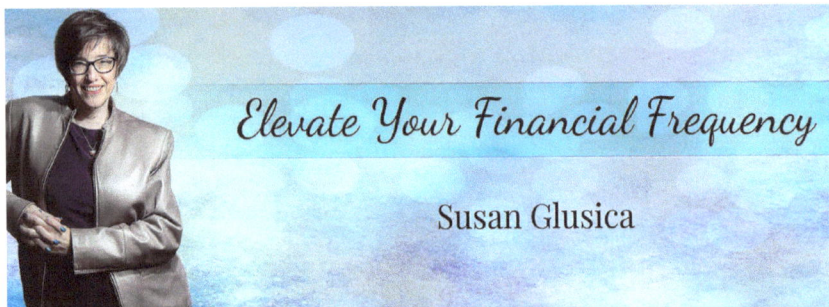

Elevate Your Financial Frequency

Susan Glusica

My name is Susan Glusica. I am the UNRIVALED REALIZER. I am known for humanizing the fastest path to inviting in and receiving more money because I am a stand for UNAPOLOGETIC PROSPERITY. What I want for myself I want for everyone! My clients expand their prosperity, generosity and legacy…without more bandwidth, working longer/harder, or inconsistent results.

After 20 years in the "corporate cubicle" side of the financial services industry, I had a crisis of legacy and could no longer see my impact in the world. I wanted proximity with clients. I wanted to make a bigger, bolder difference in my life and the lives of others.

After 8 years on the client-facing side, I realized, no matter their income level, the biggest money challenge people face is being unaware how to keep, give and grow more so they can be, do and have more.

In 2018, I founded Unrivaled Realizations LLC and created my signature group coaching program, Money Realities & Realizations. Through my discovery of the **7 Money Realities**, I created a powerfully practical method for attracting and realizing more money. In 2019 I innovated a quick results program to add $8,000+ to your bank account in thirty days or sooner. In 2020 I added ninety-minute "Money Innovation Sessions" to quickly identify top three ways to add $3,000+ to your life.

I co-hosted a popular 2018 WTBQ weekly radio show, "Wall Street to Main Street, Money Matters that Matter." I am a multi-time international best-selling author, a Certified Speaker by Women's Prosperity Network (WPN), Leader of WPN's Orange County Chapter 2016-2018, and member, Polka Dot Powerhouse – Diamonds (2020-2021). I gratefully support Thanksgiving Together, The Woodson Center, and USO.

I hold a Bachelor of Arts Degree in Humanities from New York University with honors. I am the proud recipient of New York University's Founder's Day Award for scholarly achievement and member, Alpha Sigma Lambda, Delta Upsilon Chapter.

I reside in the scenic four-season resort area of Northern Poconos in Pennsylvania with my husband and our cat, and enjoy local nature walks, SCUBA, and good food.

Booking Information: susan@susanglusica.com

Facebook: UnrivaledRealizations

Web: susanglusica.com

Call or Text: 1-845-238-7186

You're invited!

Receive a starter prosperity set of:

7 Prosperity Keys to Bring in More Money with Ease

In this quick action guide, you:

- Instantly receive expert action steps to easily receive more money.
- Get a BONUS of 7 Prosperity Principles you can effortlessly put into immediate practice!
- Are invited to joyously get CLARITY on what's possible for your money.

Go to susanglusica.com and ...

Access Your Gift NOW!

www.ingramcontent.com/pod-product-compliance
Lightning Source LLC
Chambersburg PA
CBHW051233090426
42740CB00001B/9